GROWING
HERBS

Tracy Nelson Maurer

GREEN THUMB
GUIDES

The Rourke Book Company, Inc.
Vero Beach, Florida 32964

Tracy Nelson Maurer specializes in nonfiction and business writing. Her most recently published children's books include the Bodyworks series, also from Rourke Publishing. A graduate of the University of Minnesota Journalism School, Tracy lives with her husband Mike and two children in Superior, Wisconsin.

With appreciation to gardeners Lois M. Nelson, Harvey Almstedt, and Lois I. Nelson; and to Richard J. Zondag, Jung Seed Company.

PHOTO CREDITS:
All photos and illustrations © East Coast Studios except p. 10, © USDA

PRODUCED & DESIGNED by East Coast Studios
eastcoaststudios.com

EDITORIAL SERVICES:
Lois M. Nelson
Pamela Schroeder

Library of Congress Cataloging-in-Publication Data

Maurer, Tracy, 1965-
   Growing herbs / Tracy Nelson Maurer.
     p. cm. — (Green thumb guides)
   Includes bibliographical references (p.).
   Summary: Describes how to plant, care for, and use various kinds of herbs.
   ISBN 1-55916-253-8
   1. Herb gardening—Juvenile literature. 2. Herbs—Juvenile literature. [1. Herb gardening. 2. Herbs. 3. Gardening.]
I. Title.

SB351 .H5 M342 2000
635'.7—dc21

00–026339

Printed in the USA

Table of Contents

Plants With a Purpose

Have you eaten pizza, pickles, or tacos? Their spicy tastes come from herbs. Herbs do even more than add flavor to food.

Think of herbs as useful plants. Some make good tea. Other herbs help sick people feel better. Early Native Americans knew how to use herbs for medicine.

Many herbs make nice smells when you crush their leaves, flowers, or roots. **Lavender** (LAV en dir) smells good and it even keeps fleas away!

Fun Fact
Americans say *ERB,* but people in England say *HERB.*

Some gardeners call the aloe plant an herb because of its many uses. A slimy, clear juice inside the plant helps heal cuts, sunburns, and dry skin.

Easy Herbs to Grow

Most herbs are easy to grow. They need very little care. Many gardeners grow some herbs outside and a few herbs in pots inside. A kitchen windowsill makes a good winter home for herbs. Cooks like to add the fresh flavors to food all year.

Oregano, parsley, and dill are three favorite herbs, or spices, for cooking.

You can find dried herbs in small spice jars at the grocery store. Spaghetti sauce often has three or more herbs in it!

Like flowers, herbs may be **perennials** (puh REN ee ulz) or **annuals** (AN you ulz). Perennials grow back every spring. Annuals die with autumn's frost. Plant both perennial and annual herbs in your garden for more variety.

Planting Plans

In the late 1800s, many gardeners planted formal herb gardens. These fancy gardens often surrounded a fountain, birdbath, or monument. Today, people plant herbs anywhere. Herbs grow outdoors next to flowers or vegetables. They grow indoors in pots.

If you plant outdoors, draw a garden plan first. Make sure that you leave room to water and weed your herbs. Put the smallest plants in front and biggest ones in back. Then all the herbs can catch plenty of sunshine.

Try To Grow These Herbs

Lavender: It smells sweet and keeps fleas off pets.

Catnip: Cats love to roll in crushed catnip. Some even eat it.

Parsley: Cooks use it for flavor in foods and to decorate plates.

Chives: "Onion grass" gives food an onion flavor.

Peppermint: This sweet taste can also help calm upset stomaches.

Formal herb gardens use circles, squares, and triangles to make neat designs. Here are two types of formal herb garden plans. Any herb garden should start with a plan.

TWO KINDS OF FORMAL HERB GARDENS

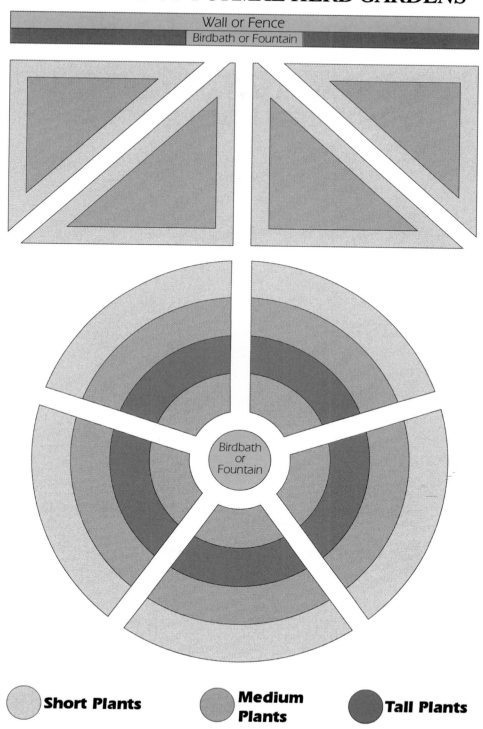

Wall or Fence

Birdbath or Fountain

Birdbath or Fountain

Short Plants   Medium Plants   Tall Plants

AVERAGE ANNUAL
MINIMUM TEMPERATURES

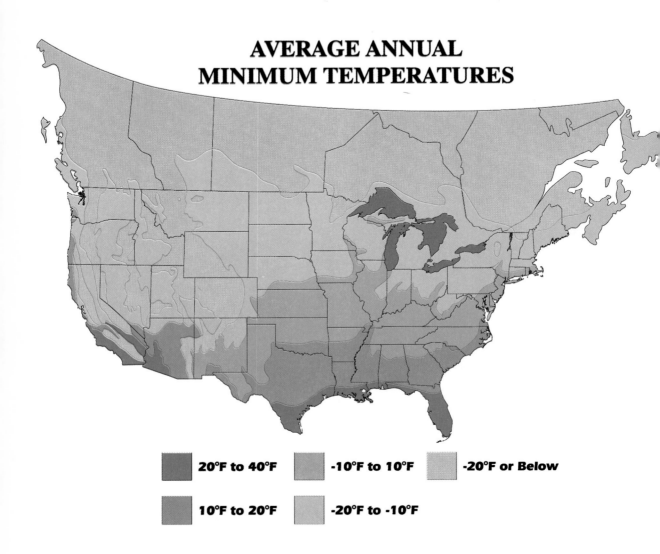

20°F to 40°F	-10°F to 10°F	-20°F or Below
10°F to 20°F	-20°F to -10°F	

Sun, Sun, Sun

Most herbs love the sun. Place potted herbs in your sunny windows. Watch your outdoor garden to see where the sun shines the most during the day. Herbs will grow well there.

Check a Plant Hardiness Zone Map like the one shown here. It will help you choose which herbs to grow where you live. Herbs such as lavender and thyme will grow as perennials where winters stay warm. However, if winter lows reach -20° Fahrenheit (-29° Celsius) or more, they will die just like annuals.

A Plant Hardiness Zone Map helps gar..eners know which plants will grow well in their area. A zone map can't always predict the weather, but it is a useful guide.

Garden Tools

Garden tools help you care for your plants. You can clean and mix soil with a rake. Use the hoe to chop clumpy soil and dig up weeds. Weeds steal water and food from your plants.

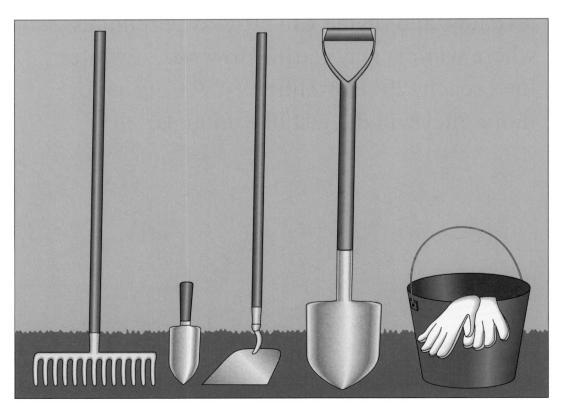

Before you start a garden, make sure you have a rake, trowel, hoe, shovel, bucket, and gloves.

Always carry garden tools with the sharp ends down.

Dig holes for planting with a trowel and shovel. You'll also want a bucket for watering plants and gloves to protect your hands.

For safety, always carry tools with the sharp ends down. Clean your tools after each use.

Make a Mud Pie

Soil carries food and water to plants. Most herbs grow best in **loam** (LOHM), or soil with large and small pieces of earth mixed with **organic matter** (or GAN ick MAT ur). A mud pie made of loam sticks together until you poke it. Then it falls apart.

Soil with too much clay makes a hard mud pie that won't fall apart. Water and food do not flow very well through clay.

Sandy soil crumbles and won't stick together. Water and food seep through sand before plant roots can soak them up.

The light brown soil (left) is too sandy. The dark brown soil (right) is loam. It helps plants grow well.

Sow the Seeds

Nurseries (NUR sur eez) sell seedlings, or baby plants. You can also sow, or plant, your own seeds.

Seed packages often show how deep to sow the seeds. Push your finger into the soil to make a hole. Put one seed in each hole. Fill the hole with soil. Pat the soil to pop air bubbles around the seed.

Be sure to water the seed. Keep it watered for the next few weeks. Watch for your new herbs to sprout!

Helpful Hint

Add a spoonful of clean sand to tiny seeds when you plant. This makes them easy to see. It also keeps the seeds from grouping together.

These seedlings came from a nursery. Hold the plants by the bottom leaves when you move them to a pot or garden.

Garden Care

Most herbs need about an inch of water each week. Potted plants dry out faster than outdoor gardens. Sometimes they need water every day.

You can check to see if the soil is too dry. Stir some soil near your plants with your finger. The soil should look dark and feel wet at least 1 inch (2.5 centimeters) deep.

Use your finger to check the soil. If it feels dry an inch down, give your plant a drink of water.

Pinch off dead leaves and flowers. This helps the plant to grow thicker stems and keep its flavor.

Pull out any weeds you see. Pinch off dead leaves and flowers.

Enjoy your garden, too. Take in the smells, sights, and sounds.

Friendly Bugs

Some insects such as ladybugs and praying mantis act like guards for your garden. They keep out harmful bugs that eat your herbs.

Herb Harvest

Harvest (HAHR vist) herbs when they stand about 5 inches (12.5 centimeters) tall. Herbs keep their flavor better if you cut young stems in the morning. Check the seed package for harvesting tips, too.

You can keep herbs to use later. Put a rubber band around a small bunch of stems. The rubber bands tighten as the herbs dry. Hang the bunch upside down to dry. A warm room like the kitchen works well.

Try This!

Add chopped chives and parsley to potatoes. Sprinkle dill on grilled cheese sandwiches or tomato soup. Put a small mint stem in your iced tea. Put lavender petals in your bath.

Many people add chives to potatoes. Chives taste a bit like onions.

GLOSSARY

annuals (AN you ulz) — plants that grow for one season and die in the fall

harvest (HAHR vist) — to pick or gather the parts of plants you can eat or use

lavender (LAV en dir) — an herb with small, purple flowers

loam (LOHM) — rich soil with large and small pieces of earth, such as clay and sand, mixed with organic matter

nurseries (NUR sur eez) — places that grow and sell seedlings, or baby plants

organic matter (or GAN ick MAT ur) — well-rotted pieces from anything that once was alive, such as old leaves, cow manure, or fish bones

perennials (puh REN ee ulz) — plants with green parts that die in the fall; the green parts grow back again from the roots in the spring

Harvest herbs when they stand about 5 inches (12.5 centimeters) tall.

INDEX

FURTHER READING

Find out more about gardening with these helpful books:
• Ambler, Wayne et al. *Treasury of Gardening.* Lincolnwood, Ill.: Publications International, 1994.
• Hart, Avery, and Paul Mantell. *Kids Garden!: The Anytime, Anyplace Guide To Sowing & Growing Fun.* Charlotte, Vermont: Williamson Publishing Co., 1996.
• *Rodale's Illustrated Encyclopedia of Gardening and Landscaping Techniques.* Edited by Barbara W. Ellis. Emmaus, Penn.: Rodale Press, 1990.

On-line resources:
Search for "kids gardening" on the World Wide Web to see many different sites.
• www.garden.org (c) National Gardening Association, 1999.